WHY I AM
NOT A CHRISTIAN
AND
WHAT I BELIEVE

First Warbler Classics Edition 2023

What I Believe first published by Kegan Paul, Trench, Trubner; Dutton,
London, New York, 1925
"Why I Am Not a Christian" was a lecture delivered at Battersea Town Hall on
March 6, 1927, under the auspices of the South London Branch of the National
Secular Society. It was issued in booklet form in 1927 by the South London
Branch of the National Secular Society and the American Association for the
Advancement of Atheism, New York
Biographical Timeline © 2023 Warbler Press

www.warblerpress.com

ISBN 978-1-962572-19-4 (paperback)
ISBN 978-1-962572-20-0 (e-book)

WHY I AM
NOT A CHRISTIAN
AND
WHAT I BELIEVE

BERTRAND RUSSELL

CONTENTS

Why I Am Not a Christian

As your Chairman has told you, the subject about which I am going to speak to you tonight is "Why I am not a Christian." Perhaps it would be as well, first of all, to try to make out what one means by the word *Christian*. It is used these days in a very loose sense by a great many people. Some people mean no more by it than a person who attempts to live a good life. In that sense I suppose there would be Christians in all sects and creeds; but I do not think that that is the proper sense of the word, if only because it would imply that all the people who are not Christians—all the Buddhists, Confucians, Mohammedans, and so on—are not trying to live a good life. I do not mean by a Christian any person who tries to live decently according to his lights. I think that you must have a certain amount of definite belief before you have a right to call yourself a Christian. The word does not have quite such a full-blooded meaning now as it had in the times of St Augustine and St Thomas Aquinas. In those days, if a man said that he was a Christian it was known what he meant. You accepted a whole collection of creeds which were set out with great precision, and every single syllable of those creeds you believed with the whole strength of your convictions.

WHAT IS A CHRISTIAN?

Nowadays it is not quite that. We have to be a little more vague in our meaning of Christianity. I think, however, that there are two different items which are quite essential to anybody calling himself a Christian. The first is one of a dogmatic nature—namely, that you must believe in God and immortality. If you do not believe in those two things, I do not think that you can properly call yourself a Christian. Then, further than that, as the name implies, you must have some kind of belief about Christ. The Mohammedans, for instance, also believe in God and in immortality, and yet they would not call themselves Christians. I think you must have at the very lowest the belief that Christ was, if not divine, at least the best and wisest of men. If you are not going to believe that much about Christ, I do not think you have any right to call yourself a Christian. Of course there is another sense which you find in *Whitaker's Almanack* and in geography books, where the population of the world is said to be divided into Christians, Mohammedans, Buddhists, fetish worshippers, and so on; and in that sense we are all Christians. The geography books count us all in, but that is a purely geographical sense, which I suppose we can ignore. Therefore I take it that when I tell you why I am not a Christian I have to tell you two different things; first, why I do not believe in God and in immortality; and, secondly, why I do not think that Christ was the best and wisest of men, although I grant Him a very high degree of moral goodness.

But for the successful efforts of unbelievers in the past, I could not take so elastic a definition of Christianity as that. As I said before, in olden days it had a much more full-blooded sense. For instance, it concluded the belief in hell. Belief in eternal hell fire was an essential item of Christian belief until pretty recent times. In this country, as you know, it ceased to be an essential item because of a decision of the Privy Council, and from that decision the Archbishop of Canterbury and the Archbishop of York dissented; but in this country our religion is settled by Act of Parliament, and therefore the Privy Council was able to override Their Graces and hell was no longer necessary to a Christian. Consequently I shall not insist that a Christian must believe in hell.

THE EXISTENCE OF GOD

To come to this question of the existence of God, it is a large and serious question, and if I were to attempt to deal with it in any adequate manner I should have to keep you here until Kingdom Come, so that you will have to excuse me if I deal with it in a somewhat summary fashion. You know, of course, that the Catholic Church has laid it down as a dogma that the existence of God can be proved by the unaided reason. That is a somewhat curious dogma, but it is one of their dogmas. They had to introduce it because at one time the Freethinkers adopted the habit of saying that there were such and such arguments which mere reason might urge against the existence of God, but of course they knew as a matter of faith that God did exist. The arguments and the reasons were set out at great length, and the Catholic Church felt that they must stop it. Therefore they laid it down that the existence of God can be proved by the unaided reason, and they had to set up what they considered were arguments to prove it. There are, of course, a number of them, but I shall take only a few.

THE FIRST-CAUSE ARGUMENT

Perhaps the simplest and easiest to understand is the argument of the First Cause. (It is maintained that everything we see in this world has a cause, and as you go back in the chain of causes further and further you must come to a First Cause, and to that First Cause you give the name of God). That argument, I suppose, does not carry very much weight nowadays, because, in the first place, cause is not quite what it used to be. The philosophers and the men of science have got going on cause, and it has not anything like the vitality it used to have; but, apart from that, you can see that the argument that there must be a First Cause is one that cannot have any validity. I may say that when I was a young man and was debating these questions very seriously in my mind, I for a long time accepted the argument of the First Cause, until one day, at the age of eighteen, I read John Stuart Mill's *Autobiography,* and I there found this sentence: "My father taught me that the question, 'Who made me?' cannot be answered, since it immediately suggests the further question, 'Who made God?'" That very simple sentence showed me, as I still think, the fallacy in the argument of the First Cause. If everything must have a cause, then God must have a cause. If there can be anything without a cause, it may just as well be the world as God, so that there cannot be any validity in that argument. It is exactly of the same nature as the Hindu's view, that the world rested upon an elephant and the elephant rested upon a tortoise; and when they said, "How about the tortoise?" the Indian said, "Suppose we change the subject." The argument is really no better than that. There is no reason why the world could not have come into being without a cause; nor, on the other hand, is there any reason why it should not have always existed. There is no reason to suppose that the world had a beginning at all. The idea that things must have a beginning is really due to the poverty of our imagination. Therefore, perhaps, I need not waste any more time upon the argument about the First Cause.

THE NATURAL LAW ARGUMENT

Then there is a very common argument from natural law.

That was a favourite argument all through the eighteenth century, especially under the influence of Sir Isaac Newton and his cosmogony. People observed the planets going round the sun according to the law of gravitation, and they thought that God had given a behest to these planets to move in that particular fashion, and that was why they did so. That was, of course, a convenient and simple explanation that saved them the trouble of looking any further for explanations of the law of gravitation. Nowadays we explain the law of gravitation in a somewhat complicated fashion that Einstein has introduced. I do not propose to give you a lecture on the law of gravitation as interpreted by Einstein, because that again would take some time; at any rate, you no longer have the sort of natural law that you had in the Newtonian system, where, for some reason that nobody could understand, nature behaved in a uniform fashion. We now find that a great many things we thought were natural laws are really human conventions. You know that even in the remotest depths of stellar space there are still three feet to a yard. That is, no doubt, a very remarkable fact, but you would hardly call it a law of nature. And a great many things that have been regarded as laws of nature are of that kind. On the other hand, where you can get down to any knowledge of what atoms actually do, you will find they are much less subject to law than people thought, and that the laws at which you arrive are statistical averages of just the sort that would emerge from chance. There is, as we all know, a law that if you throw dice you will get double sixes only about once in thirty-six times, and we do not regard that as evidence that the fall of the dice is regulated by design; on the contrary, if the double sixes came every time we should think that there was design. The laws of nature are of that sort as regards a great many of them. They are statistical averages such as would emerge from the laws of chance; and that makes this whole business of natural law much less impressive than it formerly was. Quite apart from that, which represents the momentary state of science that may change tomorrow, the whole idea that natural laws imply a law-giver is due to a confusion between natural and human laws. Human laws are behests commanding you to behave a certain way, in which way you may choose to behave, or you may choose not to behave; but natural laws are a description of how things do in fact behave, and being a mere description of what they in fact do, you cannot argue that there must be somebody who told them to do that, because even supposing that there were you are then faced with the question, "Why did God issue just those natural laws and no others?" If you say that He did it simply from His own good pleasure, and without any reason, you then find that there is something which is not subject to law, and so your train of natural law is interrupted. If you say, as more orthodox theologians do, that in all the laws which God issues He had a reason for giving those laws rather than others—the reason, of course, being to create the best universe, although you would never think it to look at it—if there was a reason for the laws which God gave, then God Himself was subject to law, and therefore you do not get any advantage by introducing God as an intermediary. You have really a law outside and anterior to the divine edicts, and God does not serve your purpose, because He is not the ultimate lawgiver. In short, this whole argument about natural law no longer has anything like the strength that it used to have. I am travelling on in time in my review of the arguments. The arguments that are used for the existence of God change their character as time goes on. They were at first hard, intellectual arguments embodying certain quite definite fallacies. As we come to modern times they become less respectable intellectually and more and more affected by a kind of moralising vagueness.

THE ARGUMENT FROM DESIGN

The next step in this process brings us to the argument from design. You all know the argument from design: everything in the world is made just so that we can manage to live in the world, and if the world was ever so little different we could not manage to live in it. That is the argument from design. It sometimes takes a rather curious form; for instance, it is argued that rabbits have white tails in order to be easy to shoot. I do not know how rabbits would view that application. It is an easy argument to parody. You all know Voltaire's remark, that obviously the nose was designed to be such as to fit spectacles. That sort of parody has turned out to be not nearly so wide of the mark as it might have seemed in the eighteenth century, because since the time of Darwin we understand much better why living creatures are adapted to their environment. It is not that their environment was made to be suitable to them, but that they grew to be suitable to it, and that is the basis of adaptation. There is no evidence of design about it.

When you come to look into this argument from design, it is a most astonishing thing that people can believe that this world, with all the things that are in it, with all its defects, should be the best that omnipotence and omniscience has been able to produce in millions of years. I really cannot believe it. Do you think that, if you were granted omnipotence and omniscience and millions of years in which to perfect your world, you could produce nothing better than the Ku-Klux-Klan or the Fascisti? Moreover, if you accept the ordinary laws of science, you have to suppose that human life and life in general on this planet will die out in due course: it is a stage in the decay of the solar system; at a certain stage of decay you get the sort of conditions of temperature and so forth which are suitable to protoplasm, and there is life for a short time in the life of the whole solar system. You see in the moon the sort of thing to which the earth is tending—something dead, cold, and lifeless.

I am told that that sort of view is depressing, and people will sometimes tell you that if they believed that they would not be able to go on living. Do not believe it; it is all nonsense. Nobody really worries much about what is going to happen millions of years hence. Even if they think they are worrying much about that, they are really deceiving themselves. They are worried about something much more mundane, or it may merely be a bad digestion; but nobody is really seriously rendered unhappy by the thought of something that is going to happen to this world millions of years hence. Therefore, although it is of course a gloomy view to suppose that life will die out—at least I suppose we may say so, although sometimes when I contemplate the things that people do with their lives I think it is almost a consolation—it is not such as to render life miserable. It merely makes you turn your attention to other things.

THE MORAL ARGUMENTS FOR THE DEITY

Now we reach one stage further in what I shall call the intellectual descent that the Theists have made in their argumentations, and we come to what are called the moral arguments for the existence of God. You all know, of course, that there used to be in the old days three intellectual arguments for the existence of God, all of which were disposed of by Immanuel Kant in the *Critique of Pure Reason;* but no sooner had he disposed of those arguments than he invented a new one, a moral argument, and that quite convinced him. He was like many people: in intellectual matters he was sceptical, but in moral matters he believed implicitly in the maxims that he had imbibed at his mother's knee. That illustrates what the psychoanalysts so much emphasise—the immensely stronger hold upon us that our very early associations have than those of later times.

Kant, as I say, invented a new moral argument for the existence of God, and that in varying forms was extremely popular during the nineteenth century. It has all sorts of forms. One form is to say that there would be no right or wrong unless God existed. I am not for the moment concerned with whether there is a difference between right and wrong, or whether there is not: that is another question. The point I am concerned with is that, if you are quite sure there is a difference between right and wrong, you are then in this situation: is that difference due to God's fiat or is it not? If it is due to God's fiat, then for God Himself there is no difference between right and wrong, and it is no longer a significant statement to say that God is good. If you are going to say, as theologians do, that God is good, you must then say that right and wrong have some meaning which is independent of God's fiat, because God's fiats are good and not bad independently of the mere fact that He made them. If you are going to say that, you will then have to say that it is not only through God that right and wrong came into being, but that they are in their essence logically anterior to God. You could, of course, if you liked, say that there was a superior deity who gave orders to the God who made this world, or could take up the line that some of the gnostics took up—a line which I often thought was a very plausible one—that as a matter of fact this world that we know was made by the devil at a moment when God was not looking. There is a good deal to be said for that, and I am not concerned to refute it.

THE ARGUMENT FOR THE REMEDYING OF INJUSTICE

Then there is another very curious form of moral argument, which is this: they say that the existence of God is required in order to bring justice into the world. In the part of this universe that we know there is great injustice, and often the good suffer, and often the wicked prosper, and one hardly knows which of those is the more annoying; but if you are going to have justice in the universe as a whole you have to suppose a future life to redress the balance of life here on earth. So they say that there must be a God, and there must be heaven and hell in order that in the long run there may be justice. That is a very curious argument. If you looked at the matter from a scientific point of view, you would say: "After all, I know only this world. I do not know about the rest of the universe, but so far as one can argue at all on probabilities one would say that probably this world is a fair sample, and if there is injustice here the odds are that there is injustice elsewhere also." Supposing you got a crate of oranges that you opened, and you found all the top layer of oranges bad, you would not argue: "The underneath ones must be good, so as to redress the balance." You would say: "Probably the whole lot is a bad consignment"; and that is really what a scientific person would argue about the universe. He would say: "Here we find in this world a great deal of injustice and so far as that goes that is a reason for supposing that justice does not rule in the world; and therefore so far as it goes it affords a moral argument against deity and not in favour of one." Of course I know that the sort of intellectual arguments that I have been talking to you about are not what really moves people. What really moves people to believe in God is not any intellectual argument at all. Most people believe in God because they have been taught from early infancy to do it, and that is the main reason.

Then I think that the next most powerful reason is the wish for safety, a sort of feeling that there is a big brother who will look after you. That plays a very profound part in influencing people's desire for a belief in God.

THE CHARACTER OF CHRIST

I now want to say a few words upon a topic which I often think is not quite sufficiently dealt with by Rationalists, and that is the question whether Christ was the best and the wisest of men. It is generally taken for granted that we shall all agree that that was so. I do not myself. I think that there are a good many points upon which I agree with Christ a great deal more than the professing Christians do. I do not know that I could go with Him all the way, but I could go with Him much farther than most professing Christians can. You will remember that He said: "Resist not evil, but whosoever shall smite thee on thy right cheek, turn to him the other also." That is not a new precept or a new principle. It was used by Lao-Tze and Buddha some five or six hundred years before Christ, but it is not a principle which as a matter of fact Christians accept. I have no doubt that the present Prime Minister,[1] for instance, is a most sincere Christian, but I should not advise any of you to go and smite him on one cheek. I think you might find that he thought this text was intended in a figurative sense.

Then there is another point which I consider is excellent. You will remember that Christ said: "Judge not lest ye be judged." That principle I do not think you would find was popular in the law courts of Christian countries. I have known in my time quite a number of judges who were very earnest Christians, and they none of them felt that they

---

1 Stanley Baldwin.

were acting contrary to Christian principles in what they did. Then Christ says: "Give to him that asketh thee, and from him that would borrow of thee turn not thou away." That is a very good principle.

Your Chairman has reminded you that we are not here to talk politics, but I cannot help observing that the last general election was fought on the question of how desirable it was to turn away from him that would borrow of thee, so that one must assume that the Liberals and Conservatives of this country are composed of people who do not agree with the teaching of Christ, because they certainly did very emphatically turn away on that occasion.

Then there is one other maxim of Christ which I think has a great deal in it, but I do not find that it is very popular among some of our Christian friends. He says: "If thou wilt be perfect, go and sell that thou hast, and give to the poor." That is a very excellent maxim, but, as I say, it is not much practised. All these, I think, are good maxims, although they are a little difficult to live up to. I do not profess to live up to them myself; but then after all, it is not quite the same thing as for a Christian.

DEFECTS IN CHRIST'S TEACHING

Having granted the excellence of these maxims, I come to certain points in which I do not believe that one can grant either the superlative wisdom or the superlative goodness of Christ as depicted in the Gospels; and here I may say that one is not concerned with the historical question. Historically it is quite doubtful whether Christ ever existed at all, and if He did we do not know anything about Him, so that I am not concerned with the historical question, which is a very difficult one. I am concerned with Christ as He appears in the Gospels, taking the Gospel narrative as it stands, and there one does find some things that do not seem to be very wise. For one thing, He certainly thought that His second coming would occur in clouds of glory before the death of all the people who were living at that time. There are a great many texts that prove that. He says, for instance: "Ye shall not have gone over the cities of Israel, till the Son of Man be come." Then He says: "There are some standing here which shall not taste death till the Son of Man comes into His kingdom"; and there are a lot of places where it is quite clear that He believed that His second coming would happen during the lifetime of many then living. That was the belief of His earlier followers, and it was the basis of a good deal of His moral teaching. When He said, "Take no thought for the morrow," and things of that sort, it was very largely because He thought that the second coming was going to be very soon, and that all ordinary mundane affairs did not count. I have, as a matter of fact, known some Christians who did believe that the second coming was imminent. I knew a parson who frightened his congregation terribly by telling them that the second coming was very imminent indeed, but they were much consoled when they found that he was planting trees in his garden. The early Christians did really believe it, and they did abstain from such things as planting trees in their gardens, because they did accept from Christ the belief that the second coming was imminent. In that respect clearly He was not so wise as some other people have been, and he was certainly not superlatively wise.

THE MORAL PROBLEM

Then you come to moral questions. There is one very serious defect to my mind in Christ's moral character, and that is that He believed in hell. I do not myself feel that any person who is really profoundly humane can believe in everlasting punishment. Christ certainly as depicted in the Gospels did believe in everlasting punishment, and one does find repeatedly a vindictive fury against those people who would not listen to His preaching—an attitude which is not uncommon with preachers, but which does somewhat detract from superlative excellence. You do not, for instance, find that attitude in Socrates. You find him quite bland and urbane towards the people who would not listen to him; and it is, to my mind, far more worthy of a sage to take that line than to take the line of indignation. You probably all remember the sort of things that Socrates was saying when he was dying, and the sort of things that he generally did say to people who did not agree with him.

You will find that in the Gospels Christ said: "Ye serpents, ye generation of vipers, how can ye escape the damnation of Hell." That was said to people who did not like His preaching. It is not really to my mind quite the best tone, and there are a great many of these things about hell. There is, of course, the familiar text about the sin against the Holy Ghost: "Whosoever speaketh against the Holy Ghost it shall not be forgiven him neither in this world nor in the world of come." That text has caused an unspeakable amount of misery in the world, for all sorts of people have imagined that they have committed the sin against the Holy Ghost, and thought that it would not be forgiven them either in this world or in the world to come. I really do not think that a person with a proper degree of kindliness in his nature would have put fears and terrors of that sort into the world.

Then Christ says: "The Son of Man shall send forth His angels, and they shall gather out of His kingdom all things that offend, and them which do iniquity, and shall cast them into a furnace of fire; there shall be wailing and gnashing of teeth"; and He goes on about the wailing and gnashing of teeth. It comes in one verse after another, and it is quite manifest to the reader that there is a certain pleasure in contemplating wailing and gnashing of teeth, or else it would not occur so often. Then you all, of course, remember about the sheep and the goats; how at the second coming to divide the sheep and the goats He is going to say to the goats: "Depart from me, ye cursed, into everlasting fire." He continues: "And these shall go away into everlasting fire." Then He says again: "If thy hand offend thee, cut it off; it is better for thee to enter into life maimed, than having two hands to go into hell, into the fire that never shall be quenched; where the worm dieth not and the fire is not quenched." He repeats that again and again also. I must say that I think all this doctrine, that hell-fire is a punishment for sin, is a doctrine of cruelty. It is a doctrine that put cruelty into the world and gave the world generations of cruel torture; and the Christ of the Gospels, if you could take Him as His chroniclers represent Him, would certainly have to be considered partly responsible for that.

There are other things of less importance. There is the instance of the Gadarene swine where it certainly was not very kind to the pigs to put the devils into them and make them rush down the hill to the sea. You must remember that He was omnipotent, and He could have made the devils simply go away; but He chooses to send them into the pigs. Then there is the curious story of the fig-tree, which always rather puzzled me. You remember what happened about the fig-tree.

He was hungry; and seeing a fig-tree afar off having leaves, He came if haply He might find anything thereon; and when He came to it He found nothing but leaves, for the time of figs was not yet. And Jesus answered and said unto it: "No man eat fruit of thee

> hereafter for ever,"…and Peter…saith unto Him: "Master, behold the fig-tree which thou cursedst is withered away."

That is a very curious story, because it was not the right time of year for figs, and you really could not blame the tree. I cannot myself feel that either in the matter of wisdom or in the matter of virtue Christ stands quite as high as some other people known to history. I think I should put Buddha and Socrates above Him in those respects.

THE EMOTIONAL FACTOR

As I said before, I do not think that the real reason why people accept religion has anything to do with argumentation. They accept religion on emotional grounds. One is often told that it is a very wrong thing to attack religion, because religion makes men virtuous. So I am told; I have not noticed it. You know, of course, the parody of that argument in Samuel Butler's book, *Erewhon Revisited.* You will remember that in *Erewhon* there is a certain Higgs who arrives in a remote country, and after spending some time there he escapes from that country in a balloon. Twenty years later he comes back to that country and finds a new religion, in which he is worshipped under the name of the "Sun Child," and it is said that he ascended into Heaven. He finds that the Feast of the Ascension is about to be celebrated, and he hears Professors Hanky and Panky say to each other that they never set eyes on the man Higgs, and they hope they never will; but they are the high priests of the religion of the Sun Child. He is very indignant, and he comes up to them, and he says: "I am going to expose all this humbug and tell the people of Erewhon that it was only I, the man Higgs, and I went up in a balloon." He was told: "You must not do that, because all the morals of this country are bound round this myth, and if they once know that you did not ascend into heaven they will all become wicked"; and so he is persuaded of that and he goes quietly away.

That is the idea—that we should all be wicked if we did not hold to the Christian religion. It seems to me that the people who have held to it have been for the most part extremely wicked. You find this curious fact, that the more intense has been the religion of any period and the more profound has been the dogmatic belief, the greater has been the cruelty and the worse has been the state of affairs. In the so-called ages of faith, when men really did believe the Christian religion in all its completeness, there was the Inquisition, with its tortures; there were millions of unfortunate women burnt as witches; and there was every kind of cruelty practised upon all sorts of people in the name of religion.

You find as you look around the world that every single bit of progress in humane feeling, every improvement in the criminal law, every step towards the diminution of war, every step towards better treatment of the coloured races, or every mitigation of slavery, every moral progress that there has been in the world, has been consistently opposed by the organised Churches of the world. I say quite deliberately that the Christian religion, as organised in its Churches, has been and still is the principal enemy of moral progress in the world.

HOW THE CHURCHES HAVE RETARDED PROGRESS

You may think that I am going too far when I say that that is still so. I do not think that I am. Take one fact. You will bear with me if I mention it. It is not a pleasant fact, but the

Churches compel one to mention facts that are not pleasant. Supposing that in this world that we live in today an inexperienced girl is married to a syphilitic man, in that case the Catholic Church says: "This is an indissoluble sacrament. You must stay together for life." And no steps of any sort must be taken by that woman to prevent herself from giving birth to syphilitic children. That is what the Catholic Church says. I say that that is fiendish cruelty, and nobody whose natural sympathies have not been warped by dogma, or whose moral nature was not absolutely dead to all sense of suffering, could maintain that it is right and proper that that state of things should continue.

That is only an example. There are a great many ways in which at the present moment the Church, by its insistence upon what it chooses to call morality, inflicts upon all sorts of people undeserved and unnecessary suffering. And of course, as we know, it is in its major part an opponent still of progress and of improvement in all the ways that diminish suffering in the world, because it has chosen to label as morality a certain narrow set of rules of conduct which have nothing to do with human happiness; and when you say that this or that ought to be done because it would make for human happiness, they think that has nothing to do with the matter at all. "What has human happiness to do with morals? The object of morals is not to make people happy."

FEAR THE FOUNDATION OF RELIGION

Religion is based, I think, primarily and mainly upon fear. It is partly the terror of the unknown, and partly, as I have said, the wish to feel that you have a kind of elder brother who will stand by you in all your troubles and disputes. Fear is the basis of the whole thing—fear of the mysterious, fear of defeat, fear of death. Fear is the parent of cruelty, and therefore it is no wonder if cruelty and religion has gone hand-in-hand. It is because fear is at the basis of those two things. In this world we can now begin a little to understand things, and a little to master them by help of science, which has forced its way step by step against the Christian religion, against the Churches, and against the opposition of all the old precepts. Science can help us to get over this craven fear in which mankind has lived for so many generations. Science can teach us, and I think our own hearts can teach us, no longer to look round for imaginary supports, no longer to invent allies in the sky, but rather to look to our own efforts here below to make this world a fit place to live in, instead of the sort of place that the churches in all these centuries have made it.

WHAT WE MUST DO

We want to stand upon our own feet and look fair and square at the world—its good facts, its bad facts, its beauties, and its ugliness; see the world as it is, and be not afraid of it. Conquer the world by intelligence, and not merely by being slavishly subdued by the terror that comes from it. The whole conception of God is a conception derived from the ancient Oriental despotisms. It is a conception quite unworthy of free men. When you hear people in church debasing themselves and saying that they are miserable sinners, and all the rest of it, it seems contemptible and not worthy of self-respecting human beings. We ought to stand up and look the world frankly in the face. We ought to make the best we can of the world, and if it is not so good as we wish, after all it will still be better than what these others have made of it in all these ages. A good world needs knowledge, kindliness, and courage; it does not need a regretful hankering after the past, or a fettering of the free intelligence by the words uttered long ago by ignorant men. It needs a fearless outlook and a free intelligence. It needs hope for the future, not looking back all the time towards a past that is dead, which we trust will be far surpassed by the future that our intelligence can create.

What I Believe

PREFACE

In this little book, I have tried to say what I think of man's place in the universe, and of his possibilities in the way of achieving the good life. In *Icarus* I expressed my fears; in the following pages I have expressed my hopes. The inconsistency is only apparent. Except in astronomy, mankind have not achieved the art of predicting the future; in human affairs, we can see that there are forces making for happiness, and forces making for misery. We do not know which will prevail, but to act wisely we must be aware of both.

January, 1st 1925

B. R.

1

NATURE AND MAN

MAN IS A part of Nature, not something contrasted with Nature. His thoughts and his bodily movements follow the same laws that describe the motions of stars and atoms. The physical world is large compared with Man—larger than it was thought to be in Dante's time, but not so large as it seemed a hundred years ago. Both upward and downward, both in the large and in the small, science seems to be reaching limits. It is thought that the universe is of finite extent in space, and that light could travel round it in a few hundred millions of years. It is thought matter consists of electrons and protons, which are of finite size and of which there are only a finite number in the world. Probably their changes are not continuous, as used to be thought, but proceed by jerks, which are never smaller than a certain minimum jerk. The laws of these changes can apparently be summed up in a small number of very general principles, which determine the past and the future of the world when any small section of its history is known.

Physical science is thus approaching the stage when it will be complete, and therefore uninteresting. Given the laws governing the motions of electrons and protons, the rest is merely geography—a collection of particular facts telling their distribution throughout some portion of the world's history. The total number of facts of geography required to determine the world's history is probably finite; theoretically they could all be written down in a big book to be kept at Somerset House with a calculating machine attached which, by turning a handle, would enable the inquirer to find out the facts at other times than those recorded. It is difficult to imagine anything less interesting or more different from the passionate delights of incomplete discovery. It is like climbing a high mountain and finding nothing at the top except a restaurant where they sell ginger beer, surrounded by fog but equipped with wireless. Perhaps in the times of Ahmes the multiplication table was exciting.

Of this physical world, uninteresting in itself, Man is a part. His body, like other matter, is composed of electrons and protons, which, so far as we know, obey the same laws as those not forming part of animals or plants. There are some who maintain that physiology can never be reduced to physics, but their arguments are not very convincing and it seems prudent to suppose that they are mistaken. What we call our "thoughts" seem to depend upon the organisation of tracks in the brain in the same sort of way in which journeys depend upon roads and railways. The energy used in thinking seems to have a chemical origin; for instance, a deficiency of iodine will turn a clever man into an idiot. Mental phenomena seem to be bound up with material structure. If this be so, we cannot suppose that a solitary electron or proton can "think"; we might as well expect a solitary individual to play a football match. We also cannot suppose that an individual's thinking survives bodily death, since that destroys the organisation of the brain, and dissipates the energy which utilised the brain tracks.

God and immortality, the central dogmas of the Christian religion, find no support in science. It cannot be said that either doctrine is essential to religion, since neither is found in Buddhism. (With regard to immortality, this statement in an unqualified form might be misleading, but it is correct in the last analysis.) But we in the West have come to think of them as the irreducible minimum of theology. No doubt people will continue to entertain these beliefs, because they are pleasant, just as it is pleasant to think ourselves virtuous and our enemies wicked. But for my part I cannot see any ground for either. I do not pretend to be able to prove that there is no God. I equally cannot prove that Satan is a fiction. The Christian God may exist; so may the Gods of Olympus, or of ancient Egypt, or of Babylon. But no one of these hypotheses is more probable than any other: they lie outside the region of even probable knowledge, and therefore there is no reason to consider any of them. I shall not enlarge upon this question, as I have dealt with it elsewhere.[1]

The question of personal immortality stands on a somewhat different footing. Here evidence either way is possible. Persons are part of the everyday world with which science is concerned, and the conditions which determine their existence are discoverable. A drop of water is not immortal; it can be resolved into oxygen and hydrogen. If, therefore, a drop of water were to maintain that it had a quality of aqueousness which would survive its dissolution we should be inclined to be sceptical. In like manner we know that the brain is not immortal, and that the organised energy of a living body becomes, as it were, demobilised at death, and therefore not available for collective action. All the evidence goes to show that what we regard as our mental life is bound up with brain structure and organised bodily energy. Therefore it is rational to suppose that mental life

---

1 See my *Philosophy of Leibniz,* Chapter XV.

ceases when bodily life ceases. The argument is only one of probability, but it is as strong as those upon which most scientific conclusions are based.

There are various grounds upon which this conclusion might be attacked. Psychical research professes to have actual scientific evidence of survival, and undoubtedly its procedure is, in principle, scientifically correct. Evidence of this sort might be so overwhelming that no one with a scientific temper could reject it. The weight to be attached to the evidence, however, must depend upon the antecedent probability of the hypothesis of survival. There are always different ways of accounting for any set of phenomena and of these we should prefer the one which is antecedentally least improbable. Those who already think it likely that we survive death will be ready to view this theory as the best explanation of psychical phenomena. Those who, on other grounds, regard this theory as implausible will seek for other explanations. For my part, I consider the evidence so far adduced by psychical research in favour of survival much weaker than the physiological evidence on the other side. But I fully admit that it might at any moment become stronger, and in that case it would be unscientific to disbelieve in survival.

Survival of bodily death is, however, a different matter from immortality: it may only mean a postponement of psychical death. It is immortality that men desire to believe in. Believers in immortality will object to physiological arguments, such as I have been using, on the ground that soul and body are totally disparate, and that the soul is something quite other than its empirical manifestations through our bodily organs. I believe this to be a metaphysical superstition. Mind and matter alike are for certain purposes convenient terms, but are not ultimate realities. Electrons and protons, like the soul, are logical fictions; each is really a history, a series of events, not a single persistent entity. In the case of the soul, this is obvious from the facts of growth. Whoever considers conception, gestation, and infancy cannot seriously believe that the soul in any indivisible something, perfect and complete throughout this process. It is evident that it grows like the body, and that it derives both from the spermatozoon and from the ovum, so that it cannot be indivisible. This is not materialism: it is merely the recognition that everything interesting is a matter of organisation, not of primal substance.

Metaphysicians have advanced innumerable arguments to prove that the soul *must* be immortal. There is one simple test by which all these arguments can be demolished. They all prove equally that the soul must pervade all space. But as we are not so anxious to be fat as to live long, none of the metaphysicians in question have ever noticed this application of their reasonings. This is an instance of the amazing power of desire in blinding even very able men to fallacies which would otherwise be obvious at once. If we were not afraid of death, I do not believe that the idea of immortality would ever have arisen.

Fear is the basis of religious dogma, as of so much else in human life. Fear of human beings, individually or collectively, dominates much of our social life, but it is fear of nature that gives rise to religion. The antithesis of mind and matter is, as we have seen, more or less illusory; but there is another antithesis which is more important—that, namely, between things that can be affected by our desires and things that cannot be so affected. The line between the two is neither sharp nor immutable—as science advances, more and more things are brought under human control. Nevertheless there remain things definitely on the other side. Among these are all the *large* facts of our world, the sort of facts that are dealt with by astronomy. It is only facts on or near the surface of the earth that we can, to some extent, mould to suit our desires. And even on the surface of the earth our powers are very limited. Above all, we cannot prevent death, although we can often delay it.

Religion is an attempt to overcome this antithesis. If the world is controlled by God, and God can be moved by prayer, we acquire a share in omnipotence. In former days, miracles happened in answer to prayer; they still do in the Catholic Church, but Protestants have lost this power. However, it is possible to dispense with miracles, since Providence has decreed that the operation of natural laws shall produce the best possible results. Thus belief in God still serves to humanise the world of nature, and to make men feel that physical forces are really their allies. In like manner immortality removes the terror from death. People who believe that when they die they will inherit eternal bliss may be expected to view death without horror, though, fortunately for medical men, this does not invariably happen. It does, however, soothe men's fears somewhat even when it cannot allay them wholly.

Religion, since it has its source in terror, has dignified certain kinds of fear, and made people think them not disgraceful. In this it has done mankind a great disservice: *all* fear is bad. I believe that when I die I shall rot, and nothing of my ego will survive. I am not young, and I love life. But I should scorn to shiver with terror at the thought of annihilation. Happiness is none the less true happiness because it must come to an end, nor do thought and love lose their value because they are not everlasting. Many a man has borne himself proudly on the scaffold; surely the same pride should teach us to think truly about man's place in the world. Even if the open windows of science at first make us shiver after the cosy indoor warmth of traditional humanising myths, in the end the fresh air brings vigour, and the great spaces have a splendour of their own.

The philosophy of nature is one thing, the philosophy of value is quite another. Nothing but harm can come of confusing them. What we think good, what we should like, has no bearing whatever upon what is, which is the question for the philosophy of nature. On the other hand, we cannot be forbidden to value this or that on the ground that the nonhuman world does not value it, nor can we be compelled to admire anything because it is a "law of nature." Undoubtedly we are part of nature, which has produced our desires, our hopes and fears, in accordance with laws which the physicist is beginning to discover. In this sense we are part of nature, we are subordinated to nature, the outcome of natural laws, and their victims in the long run.

The philosophy of nature must not be unduly terrestrial; for it, the earth is merely one of the smaller planets of one of the smaller stars of the Milky Way. It would be ridiculous to warp the philosophy of nature in order to bring out results that are pleasing to the tiny parasites of this insignificant planet. Vitalism as a philosophy, and evolutionism, show, in this respect, a lack of sense of proportion and logical relevance. They regard the facts of life, which are personally interesting to us, as having a cosmic significance, not a significance confined to the earth's surface. Optimism and pessimism, as cosmic philosophies, show the same naïve humanism; the great world, so far as we know it from the philosophy of nature, is neither good nor bad, and is not concerned to make us happy or unhappy. All such philosophies spring from self-importance, and are best corrected by a little astronomy.

But in the philosophy of value the situation is reversed. Nature is only a part of what we can imagine; everything, real or imagined, can be appraised by us, and there is no outside standard to show that our valuation is wrong. We are ourselves the ultimate and irrefutable arbiters of value, and in the world of value Nature is only a part. Thus in this world we are greater than Nature. In the world of values, Nature in itself is neutral, neither good nor bad, deserving of neither admiration nor censure. It is we who create value and our desires which confer value. In this realm we are kings, and we debase our kingship if we bow down to Nature. It is for us to determine the good life, not for Nature —not even for Nature personified as God.

2

THE GOOD LIFE

THERE HAVE BEEN at different times and among different people many varying conceptions of the good life. To some extent the differences were amenable to argument; this was when men differed as to the means to achieve a given end. Some think that prison is a good way of preventing crime; others hold that education would be better. A difference of this sort can be decided by sufficient evidence. But some differences cannot be tested in this way. Tolstoy condemned all war; others have held the life of a soldier doing battle for the right to be very noble. Here there was probably involved a real difference as to ends. Those who praise the soldier usually consider the punishment of sinners a good thing in itself; Tolstoy did not think so. On such a matter no argument is possible. I cannot, therefore, prove that my view of the good life is right; I can only state my view, and hope that as many as possible will agree. My view is this:

The good life is one inspired by love and guided by knowledge.

Knowledge and love are both indefinitely extensible; therefore, however good a life may be, a better life can be imagined. Neither love without knowledge, nor knowledge without love can produce a good life. In the Middle Ages, when pestilence appeared in a country, holy men advised the population to assemble in churches and pray for deliverance; the result was that the infection spread with extraordinary rapidity among the crowded masses of supplicants. This was an example of love, without knowledge. The late war afforded an example of knowledge without love. In each case, the result was death on a large scale.

Although both love and knowledge are necessary, love is in a sense more fundamental, since it will lead intelligent people to seek knowledge, in order to find out how to benefit those whom they love. But if people are not intelligent, they will be content to believe what they have been told, and may do harm in spite of the most genuine benevolence. Medicine affords, perhaps, the best example of what I mean. An able physician is more useful to a patient than the most devoted friend, and progress in medical knowledge does more for the health of the community than ill-informed philanthropy. Nevertheless, an element of benevolence is essential even here if any but the rich are to profit by scientific discoveries.

Love is a word which covers a variety of feelings; I have used it purposely, as I wish to include them all. Love as an emotion—which is what I am speaking about, for love "on principle" does not seem to me genuine—moves between two poles: on one side, pure delight in contemplation; on the other, pure benevolence. Where inanimate objects are concerned, delight alone enters in; we cannot feel benevolence towards a landscape or a sonata. This type of enjoyment is presumably the source of art. It is stronger, as a rule, in very young children than in adults, who are apt to view objects in a utilitarian spirit. It plays a large part in our feelings towards human beings, some of whom have charm and some the reverse, when considered simply as objects of aesthetic contemplation.

The opposite pole of love is pure benevolence. Men have sacrificed their lives to helping lepers; in such a case the love they felt cannot have had any element of aesthetic delight. Parental affection, as a rule, is accompanied by pleasure in the child's appearance, but remains strong when this element is wholly absent. It would seem odd to call a mother's interest in a sick child "benevolence," because we are in the habit of using this word to describe a pale emotion nine parts humbug. But it is difficult to find any other word to describe the desire for another person's welfare. It is a fact that a desire of this sort may reach any degree of strength in the case of parental feeling. In other cases it is far less intense; indeed it would seem likely that all altruistic emotion is a sort of overflow of parental feeling, or sometimes a sublimation of it. For want of a better word, I shall call this emotion "benevolence." But I want to make it clear that I am speaking of an emotion, not a principle, and that I do not include in it any feeling of superiority such as is sometimes associated with the word. The word "sympathy" expresses part of what I mean, but leaves out the element of activity that I wish to include.

Love at its fullest is an indissoluble combination of the two elements, delight and well-wishing. The pleasure of a parent in a beautiful and successful child combines both elements; so does sex-love at its best. But in sex-love benevolence will only exist where there is secure possession, since otherwise jealousy will destroy it, while perhaps actually increasing the delight in contemplation. Delight without well-wishing may be cruel; well-wishing without delight easily tends to become cold and a little superior. A person who wishes to be loved wishes to be the object of a love containing both elements, except in cases of extreme weakness, such as infancy and severe illness. In these cases benevolence may be all that is desired. Conversely, in cases of extreme strength, admiration is more desired than benevolence: this is the state of mind of potentates and famous beauties. We only desire other people's good wishes in proportion as we feel ourselves in need of help or in danger of harm from them. At least, that would seem to be the biological logic of the situation, but it is not quite true to life. We desire affection in order to escape from the feeling of loneliness, in order to be, as we say, "understood." This is a matter of sympathy, not merely of benevolence; the person whose affection is satisfactory to us must not merely wish us well, but must know in what our happiness consists. But this belongs to the other element of the good life, namely knowledge.

In a perfect world, every sentient being would be to every other the object of the fullest love, compounded of delight, benevolence, and understanding inextricably blended. It does not follow that, in this actual world, we ought to attempt to have such feelings towards all the sentient beings whom we encounter. There are many in whom we cannot feel delight, because they are disgusting; if we were to do violence to our nature by trying to see beauties in them, we should merely blunt our susceptibilities to what we naturally find beautiful. Not to mention human beings there are fleas and bugs and lice. We should have to be as hard pressed as the Ancient Mariner before we could feel delight in contemplating these creatures. Some saints, it is true, have called them "pearls of God," but what these men delighted in was the opportunity of displaying their own sanctity.

Benevolence is easier to extend widely, but even

benevolence has its limits. If a man wished to marry a lady, we should not think the better of him for withdrawing if he found that someone else also wished to marry her: we should regard this as a fair field for competition. Yet his feelings towards a rival cannot be wholly benevolent. I think that in all descriptions of the good life here on earth we must assume a certain basis of animal vitality and animal instinct; without this, life becomes tame and uninteresting. Civilisation should be something added to this, not substituted for it; the ascetic saint and the detached sage fail in this respect to be complete human beings. A small number of them may enrich a community; but a world composed of them would die of boredom.

These considerations lead to a certain emphasis on the element of delight as an ingredient in the best love. Delight, in this actual world, is unavoidably selective, and prevents us from having the same feelings towards all mankind. When conflicts arise between delight and benevolence, they must, as a rule, be decided by a compromise, not by a complete surrender of either. Instinct has its rights, and if we do violence to it beyond a point it takes vengeance in subtle ways. Therefore in aiming at a good life the limits of human possibility must be borne in mind. Here again, however, we are brought back to the necessity of knowledge.

When I speak of knowledge as an ingredient of the good life, I am not thinking of ethical knowledge, but of scientific knowledge and knowledge of particular facts. I do not think there is, strictly speaking, such a thing as ethical knowledge. If we desire to achieve some end, knowledge may show us the means, and this knowledge may loosely pass as ethical. But I do not believe that we can decide what sort of conduct is right or wrong except by reference to its probable consequences. Given an end to be achieved, it is a question for science to discover how to achieve it. All moral rules must be tested by examining whether they tend to realise ends that we desire. I say ends that we desire, not ends that we *ought* to desire. What we "ought" to desire is merely what someone else wishes us to desire. Usually it is what the authorities wish us to desire—parents, school-masters, policemen, and judges. If you say to me "you ought to do so-and-so," the motive power of your remark lies in my desire for your approval—together, possibly, with rewards or punishments attached to your approval or disapproval. Since all behaviour springs from desire, it is clear that ethical notions can have no importance except as they influence desire. They do this through the desire for approval and the fear of disapproval. These are powerful social forces, and we shall naturally endeavour to win them to our side if we wish to realise any social purpose. When I say that the morality of conduct is to be judged by its probable consequences, I mean that I desire to see approval given to behaviour likely to realise social purposes which we desire, and disapproval to opposite behaviour. At present this is not done; there are certain traditional rules according to which approval and disapproval are meted out quite regardless of consequences. But this is a topic with which we shall deal in the next section.

The superfluity of theoretical ethics is obvious in simple cases. Suppose, for instance, your child is ill. Love makes you wish to cure it, and science tells you how to do so. There is not an intermediate stage of ethical theory, where it is demonstrated that your child had better be cured. Your act springs directly from desire for an end, together with knowledge of means. This is equally true of all acts, whether good or bad. The ends differ, and the knowledge is more adequate in some cases than in others. But there is no conceivable way of making people do things they do not wish to do. What is possible is to alter their desires by a system of rewards and penalties, among which social approval and disapproval are not the least potent. The question for the legislative moralist is, therefore: How shall this system of rewards and punishments be arranged so as to secure the maximum of what is desired by the legislative authority? If I say that the legislative authority has bad desires, I mean merely that its desires conflict with those of some section of the community to which I belong. Outside human desires there is no moral standard.

Thus, what distinguishes ethics from science is not any special kind of knowledge but merely desire. The knowledge required in ethics is exactly like the knowledge elsewhere; what is peculiar is that certain ends are desired, and that right conduct is what conduces to them. Of course, if the definition of right conduct is to make a wide appeal, the ends must be such as large sections of mankind desire. If I defined right conduct as that which increases my own income, readers would disagree. The whole effectiveness of any ethical argument lies in its scientific part, i.e. in the proof that one kind of conduct, rather than some other, is a means to an end which is widely desired. I distinguish, however, between ethical argument and ethical education. The latter consists in strengthening certain desires and weakening others. This is quite a different process, which will be separately discussed at a later stage.

We can now explain more exactly the purport of the definition of the good life with which this chapter began. When I said that the good life consists of love guided by knowledge, the desire which prompted me was the desire to live such a life as far as possible, and to see others living it; and the logical content of the statement is that, in a community where men live in this way, more desires will be satisfied than in one where there is less love or less knowledge. I do not mean that such a life is "virtuous" or that its opposite is "sinful," for these are conceptions which seem to me to have no scientific justification.

3

MORAL RULES

THE PRACTICAL NEED of morals arises from the conflict of desires, whether of different people or of the same person at different times or even at one time. A man desires to drink, and also to be fit for his work next morning. We think him immoral if he adopts the course which gives him the smaller total satisfaction of desire. We think ill of people who are extravagant or reckless, even if they injure no one but themselves. Bentham supposed that the whole of morality could be derived from "enlightened self-interest," and that a person who always acted with a view to his own maximum satisfaction in the long run would always act rightly. I cannot accept this view. Tyrants have existed who derived exquisite pleasure from watching the infliction of torture; I cannot praise such men when prudence led them to spare their victims' lives with a view to further sufferings another day. Nevertheless, other things being equal, prudence is a part of the good life. Even Robinson Crusoe had occasion to practise industry, self-control and foresight which must be reckoned as moral qualities, since they increased his total satisfaction without counterbalancing injury to others. This part of morals plays a great part in the training of young children, who have little inclination to think of the future. If it were more practised in later life, the world would quickly become a paradise, since it would be quite sufficient to prevent wars, which are acts of passion, not reason. Nevertheless, in spite of the importance of prudence, it is not the most interesting part of morals. Nor is it the part that raises intellectual problems, since it does not require an appeal to anything beyond self-interest.

The part of morality that is not included in prudence, is, in essence, analogous to law, or the rules of a club. It is a method of enabling men to live together in a community in spite of the possibility that their desires may conflict. But here two very different methods are possible. There is the method of criminal law, which aims at a merely external harmony by attaching disagreeable consequences to acts which thwart other men's desires in certain ways. This is also the method of social censure: to be thought ill of by one's own society is a form of punishment, to avoid which most people avoid being known to transgress the code of their set. But there is another method, more fundamental, and far more satisfactory when it succeeds. This is to alter men's characters and desires in such a way as to minimise occasions of conflict by making the success of one man's desires as far as possible consistent with that of another's. That is why love is better than hate, because it brings harmony instead of conflict into the desires of the person concerned. Two people between whom there is love succeed or fail together, but when two people hate each other the success of either is the failure of the other.

If we were right in saying that the good life is inspired by love and guided by knowledge, it is clear that the moral code of any community is not ultimate and self-sufficient, but must be examined with a view to seeing whether it is such as wisdom and benevolence would have decreed. Moral codes have not always been faultless. The Aztecs considered it their painful duty to eat human flesh for fear the light of the sun should grow dim. They erred in their science; and perhaps they would have perceived the scientific error if they had had any love for the sacrificial victims. Some tribes immure girls in the dark from the age of 10 to the age of 17, for fear the sun's rays should render them pregnant. But surely our modern codes of morals contain nothing analogous to these savage practices? Surely we only forbid things which are really harmful, or at any rate so abominable that no decent person could defend them? I am not so sure.

Current morality is a curious blend of utilitarianism and superstition, but the superstitious part has the stronger hold, as is natural, since superstition is the origin of moral rules. Originally, certain acts were thought displeasing to the gods, and were forbidden by law because the divine wrath was apt to descend upon the community, not merely upon the guilty individuals. Hence arose the conception of sin, as that which is displeasing to God. No reason can be assigned as to why certain acts should be thus displeasing; it would be very difficult to say, for instance, why it was displeasing that the kid should be seethed in its mother's milk. But it was known by Revelation that this was the case. Sometimes the Divine commands have been curiously interpreted. For example, we are told not to work on Saturdays, and Protestants take this to mean that we are not to play on Sundays. But the same sublime authority is attributed to the new prohibition as to the old.

It is evident that a man with a scientific outlook on life cannot let himself be intimidated by texts of Scripture or by the teaching of the Church. He will not be content to say "such-and-such an act is sinful, and that ends the matter."

He will inquire whether it does any harm or whether, on the contrary, the belief that it is sinful does harm. And he will find that, especially in what concerns sex, our current morality contains a very great deal of which the origin is purely superstitious. He will find also that this superstition, like that of the Aztecs, involves needless cruelty, and would be swept away if people were actuated by kindly feelings towards their neighbours. But the defenders of traditional morality are seldom people with warm hearts, as may be seen from the love of militarism displayed by Church dignitaries. One is tempted to think that they value morals as affording a legitimate outlet for their desire to inflict pain; the sinner is fair game, and therefore away with tolerance!

Let us follow an ordinary human life from conception to the grave, and note the points where superstitious morals inflict preventable suffering. I begin with conception, because here the influence of superstition is particularly noteworthy. If the parents are not married, the child has a stigma, as clearly undeserved as anything could be. If either of the parents has venereal disease, the child is likely to inherit it. If they already have too many children for the family income, there will be poverty, underfeeding, overcrowding, very likely incest. Yet the great majority of moralists agree that the parents had better not know how to prevent this misery by preventing conception. To please these moralists, a life of torture is inflicted upon millions of human beings who ought never to have existed, merely because it is supposed that sexual intercourse is wicked unless accompanied by desire for offspring, but not wicked when this desire is present, even though the offspring is humanly certain to be wretched. To be killed suddenly and then eaten, which was the fate of the Aztecs' victims, is a far less degree of suffering than is inflicted upon a child born in miserable surroundings and tainted with venereal disease.

Yet it is the greater suffering which is deliberately inflicted by bishops and politicians in the name of morality. If they had even the smallest spark of love or pity for children they could not adhere to a moral code involving this fiendish cruelty.

At birth, and in early infancy, the average child suffers more from economic causes than from superstition. When well-to-do women have children, they have the best doctors, the best nurses, the best diet, the best rest and the best exercise. Working-class women do not enjoy these advantages, and frequently their children die for lack of them. A little is done by the public authorities in the way of care of mothers, but very grudgingly. At a moment when the supply of milk to nursing mothers is being cut down to save expense, public authorities will spend vast sums on paving rich residential districts where there is little traffic. They must know that in taking this decision they are condemning a certain number of working-class children to death for the crime of poverty. Yet the ruling party are supported by the immense majority of ministers of religion, who, with the Pope at their head, have pledged the vast forces of superstition throughout the world to the support of social injustice.

In all stages of education the influence of superstition is disastrous. A certain percentage of children have the habit of thinking; one of the aims of education is to cure them of this habit. Inconvenient questions are met with "hush, hush," or with punishment. Collective emotion is used to instil certain kinds of belief, more particularly nationalistic kinds. Capitalists, militarists, and ecclesiastics co-operate in education, because all depend for their power upon the prevalence of emotionalism and the rarity of critical judgement. With the aid of human nature, education succeeds in increasing and intensifying these propensities of the average man.

Another way in which superstition damages education is through its influence on the choice of teachers. For economic reasons, a woman teacher must not be married; for moral reasons, she must not have extra-marital sexual relations. And yet everybody who has taken the trouble to study morbid psychology knows that prolonged virginity is, as a rule, extraordinarily harmful to women, so harmful that, in a sane society, it would be severely discouraged in teachers. The restrictions imposed lead more and more to a refusal, on the part of energetic and enterprising women, to enter the teaching profession. This is all due to the lingering influence of superstitious asceticism.

At middle and upper class schools the matter is even worse. There are chapel services, and the care of morals is in the hands of clergymen. Clergymen, almost necessarily, fail in two ways as teachers of morals. They condemn acts which do not harm and they condone acts which do great harm. They all condemn sexual relations between unmarried people who are fond of each other but not yet sure that they wish to live together all their lives. Most of them condemn birth control. None of them condemns the brutality of a husband who causes his wife to die of too frequent pregnancies. I knew a fashionable clergyman whose wife had nine children in nine years. The doctors told him that if she had another she would die. Next year she had another and died. No one condemned; he retained his benefice and married again. So long as clergymen continue to condone cruelty and condemn innocent pleasure, they can only do harm as guardians of the morals of the young.

Another bad effect of superstition on education is the absence of instruction about the facts of sex. The main physiological facts ought to be taught quite simply and naturally before puberty at a time when they are not exciting. At puberty, the elements of an unsuperstitious sexual morality ought to be taught. Boys and girls should be taught that nothing can justify sexual intercourse unless there is mutual inclination. This is contrary to the teaching of the Church, which holds that, provided the parties are married and the man desires another child, sexual intercourse is justified however great may be the reluctance of the wife. Boys and girls should be taught respect for each other's liberty; they should be made to feel that nothing gives one human being rights over another, and that jealousy and possessiveness kill love. They should be taught that to bring another human being into the world is a very serious matter, only to be undertaken when the child will have a reasonable prospect of health, good surroundings, and parental care. But they should also be taught methods of birth control, so as to insure that children shall only come when they are wanted. Finally, they should be taught the dangers of venereal disease, and the methods of prevention and cure. The increase of human happiness to be expected from sex education on these lines is immeasurable.

It should be recognised that, in the absence of children, sexual relations are a purely private matter, which does not concern either the State or the neighbours. Certain forms of sex which do not lead to children are at present punished by the criminal law: this is purely superstitious, since the matter is one which affects no one except the parties directly concerned. Where there are children, it is a mistake to suppose that it is necessarily to their interest to make divorce very difficult. Habitual drunkenness, cruelty, insanity are grounds upon which divorce is necessary for the children's sake quite as much as for the sake of the wife or husband. The peculiar importance attached, at present, to adultery is quite irrational. It is obvious that many forms of misconduct are more fatal to married happiness than an occasional infidelity. Masculine insistence on a child a year, which is not conventionally misconduct or cruelty, is the most fatal of all.

Moral rules ought not to be such as to make instinctive happiness impossible. Yet that is an effect of strict monogamy in a community where the numbers of the two sexes are very unequal. Of course, under such circumstances, the moral rules are infringed. But when the rules are such that they can only be obeyed by greatly diminishing the happiness of the community, and when it is better they should be infringed than observed, surely it is time that the rules were changed. If this is not done, many people who are acting in a way not contrary to the public interest are faced with the undeserved alternative of hypocrisy or obloquy. The Church does not mind hypocrisy, which is a flattering tribute to its power; but elsewhere it has come to be recognised as an evil which we ought not lightly to inflict.

Even more harmful than theological superstition is the superstition of nationalism, of duty to one's own State and to no other. But I do not propose on this occasion to discuss the matter beyond pointing out that limitation to one's compatriots is contrary to the principle of love which we recognised as constituting the good life. It is also, of course, contrary to enlightened self-interest, since an exclusive nationalism does not pay even the victorious nations.

One other respect in which our society suffers from the theological conception of "sin" is the treatment of criminals. The view that criminals are "wicked" and "deserve" punishment is not one which a rational morality can support. Undoubtedly certain people do things which society wishes to prevent, and does right in preventing as far as possible. We may take murder as the plainest case. Obviously, if a community is to hold together and we are to enjoy its pleasures and advantages, we cannot allow people to kill each other whenever they feel an impulse to do so. But this problem should be treated in a purely scientific spirit. We should ask simply: What is the best method of preventing murder? Of two methods which are equally effective in preventing murder, the one involving least harm to the murderer is to be preferred. The harm to the murderer is wholly regrettable, like the pain of a surgical operation. It may be equally necessary, but it is not a subject for rejoicing. The vindictive feeling called "moral indignation" is merely a form of cruelty. Suffering to the criminal can never be justified by the notion of vindictive punishment. If education combined with kindness is equally effective, it is to be preferred; still more is it to be preferred if it is more effective. Of course, the prevention of crime and the punishment of crime are two different questions; the object of causing pain to the criminal is presumably deterrent. If prisons were so humanised that a prisoner got a good education for nothing, people might commit crimes in order to qualify for entrance. No doubt prison must be less pleasant than freedom; but the best way to secure this result is to make freedom more pleasant than it sometimes is at present. I do not wish, however, to embark upon the subject of Penal Reform. I merely wish to suggest that we should treat the criminal as we treat a man suffering from plague. Each is a public danger, each must have his liberty curtailed until he has ceased to be a danger. But the man suffering from plague is an object of sympathy and commiseration, whereas the criminal is an object of execration. This is quite irrational. And it is because of this difference of attitude that our prisons are so much less successful in curing criminal tendencies than our hospitals are in curing disease.

4

SALVATION: INDIVIDUAL AND SOCIAL

ONE OF THE defects of traditional religion is its individualism, and this defect belongs also to the morality associated with it. Traditionally, the religious life was, as it were, a duologue between the soul and God. To obey the will of God was virtue; and this was possible for the individual quite regardless of the state of the community. Protestant sects developed the idea of "finding salvation," but it was always present in Christian teaching. This individualism of the separate soul had its value at certain stages of history, but in the modern world we need rather a social than an individual conception of welfare. I want to consider, in this section, how this affects our conception of the good life.

Christianity arose in the Roman Empire among populations, wholly destitute of political power, whose national States had been destroyed and merged in a vast impersonal aggregate. During the first three centuries of the Christian era the individuals who adopted Christianity could not alter the social or political institutions under which they lived, although they were profoundly convinced of their badness. In these circumstances, it was natural that they should adopt the belief that an individual may be perfect in an imperfect world, and that the good life has nothing to do with this world. What I mean may become plain by comparison with Plato's Republic. When Plato wanted to describe the good life, he described a whole community, not an individual; he did so in order to define justice, which is an essentially social conception. He was accustomed to citizenship of a republic, and political responsibility was something which he took for granted. With the loss of Greek freedom comes the rise of Stoicism, which is like Christianity, and unlike Plato, in having an individualistic conception of the good life.

We, who belong to great democracies, should find a more appropriate morality in free Athens than in despotic Imperial Rome. In India, where the political circumstances are very similar to those of Judea in the time of Christ, we find Gandhi preaching a very similar morality to Christ's and being punished for it by the christianised successors of Pontius Pilate. But the more extreme Indian nationalists are not content with individual salvation: they want national salvation. In this they have taken on the outlook of the free democracies of the West. I want to suggest some respects in which this outlook, owing to Christian influences, is not yet sufficiently bold and self-conscious, but is still hampered by the belief in individual salvation.

The good life, as we conceive it, demands a multitude of social conditions, and cannot be realised without them. The good life, we said, is a life inspired by love and guided by knowledge. The knowledge required can only exist where governments or millionaires devote themselves to its discovery and diffusion. For example, the spread of cancer is alarming—what are we to do about it? At the moment, no one can answer the question for lack of knowledge;

and the knowledge is not likely to emerge except through endowed research. Again, knowledge of science, history, literature and art ought to be attainable by all who desire it; this requires elaborate arrangements on the part of public authorities, and is not to be achieved by means of religious conversion. Then there is foreign trade, without which half the inhabitants of Great Britain would starve; and if we were starving very few of us would live the good life. It is needless to multiply examples. The important point is that, in all that differentiates between a good life and a bad one, the world is a unity, and the man who pretends to live independently is a conscious or unconscious parasite.

The idea of individual salvation, with which the early Christians consoled themselves for their political subjection, becomes impossible as soon as we escape from a very narrow conception of the good life. In the orthodox Christian conception, the good life is the virtuous life, and virtue consists in obedience to the will of God, and the will of God is revealed to each individual through the voice of conscience. This whole conception is that of men subject to an alien despotism. The good life involves much beside virtue—intelligence, for instance. And conscience is a most fallacious guide, since it consists of vague reminiscences of precepts heard in early youth, so that it is never wiser than its possessor's nurse or mother. To live a good life in the fullest sense a man must have a good education, friends, love, children (if he desires them), a sufficient income to keep him from want and grave anxiety, good health, and work which is not uninteresting. All these things, in varying degrees, depend upon the community, and are helped or hindered by political events. The good life must be lived in a good society, and is not fully possible otherwise.

This is the fundamental defect of the aristocratic ideal. Certain good things, such as art and science and friendship, can flourish very well in an aristocratic society. They existed in Greece on a basis of slavery; they exist among ourselves on a basis of exploitation. But love, in the form of sympathy, or benevolence, cannot exist freely in an aristocratic society. The aristocrat has to persuade himself that the slave or proletarian or coloured man is of inferior clay, and that his sufferings do not matter. At the present moment, polished English gentlemen flog Africans so severely that they die after hours of unspeakable anguish. Even if these gentlemen are well-educated, artistic, and admirable conversationalists, I cannot admit that they are living the good life. Human nature imposes some limitation of sympathy, but not such a degree as that. In a democratically-minded society, only a maniac would behave in this way. The limitation of sympathy involved in the aristocratic ideal is its condemnation. Salvation is an aristocratic ideal, because it is individualistic. For this reason, also, the idea of personal salvation, however interpreted and expanded, cannot serve for the definition of the good life.

Another characteristic of salvation is that it results from a catastrophic change, like the conversion of St Paul. Shelley's poems afford an illustration of this conception applied to societies; the moment comes when everybody is converted, the "anarchs" fly, and "the world's great age begins anew." It may be said that a poet is an unimportant person, whose ideas are of no consequence. But I am persuaded that a large proportion of revolutionary leaders have had ideas extremely like Shelley's. They have thought that misery and cruelty and degradation were due to tyrants or priests or capitalists or Germans, and that if these sources of evil were overthrown there would be a general change of heart and we should all live happy ever after. Holding these beliefs, they have been willing to wage a "war to end war." Comparatively fortunate were those who had suffered defeat or death; those who had the misfortune to emerge victorious were reduced to cynicism and despair by the failure of all their glowing hopes. The ultimate source of these hopes was the Christian doctrine of catastrophic conversion as the road to salvation.

I do not wish to suggest that revolutions are never necessary, but I do wish to suggest that they are not short cuts to the millennium. There is no short cut to the good life, whether individual or social. To build up the good life, we must build up intelligence, self-control and sympathy. This is a quantitative matter, a matter of gradual improvement, of early training, of educational experiment. Only impatience prompts the belief in the possibility of sudden improvement. The gradual improvement that is possible, and the methods by which it may be achieved, are a matter for future science. But something can be said now. Some part of what can be said I shall try to indicate in a final section.

5

SCIENCE AND HAPPINESS

The purpose of the moralist is to improve men's behaviour. This is a laudable ambition, since their behaviour is for the most part deplorable. But I cannot praise the moralist either for the particular improvements he desires or for the methods he adopts for achieving them. His ostensible method is moral exhortation; his real method (if he is orthodox) is a system of economic rewards and punishments. The former effects nothing permanent or important; the influence of revivalists, from Savonarola downwards, has always been very transitory. The latter—the rewards and punishments—have a very considerable effect. They cause a man, for example, to prefer casual prostitutes to a quasi-permanent mistress, because it is necessary to adopt the method which is most easily concealed. They thus keep up the numbers of a very dangerous profession, and secure the prevalence of venereal disease. These are not the objects desired by the moralist, and he is too unscientific to notice that they are the objects which he actually achieves.

Is there anything better to be substituted for this unscientific mixture of preaching and bribery? I think there is.

Men's actions are harmful either from ignorance or from bad desires. "Bad" desires, when we are speaking from a social point of view, may be defined as those which tend to thwart the desires of others, or more exactly, those which thwart more desires than they assist. It is not necessary to dwell upon the harmfulness that springs from ignorance; here, more knowledge is all that is wanted, so that the road to improvement lies in more research and more education. But the harmfulness that springs from bad desires is a more difficult matter.

In the ordinary man and woman there is a certain amount of active malevolence, both special ill-will directed to particular enemies and general impersonal pleasure in the misfortunes of others. It is customary to cover this over with fine phrases; about half of conventional morality is a cloak for it. But it must be faced if the moralists' aim of improving our actions is to be achieved. It is shown in a thousand ways, great and small: in the glee with which people repeat and believe scandal, in the unkind treatment of criminals in spite of clear proof that better treatment would have more effect in reforming them, in the unbelievable barbarity with which all white races treat Negroes, and in the gusto with which old ladies and clergymen pointed out the duty of military service to young men during the War. Even children may be the objects of wanton cruelty: David Copperfield and Oliver Twist are by no means imaginary. This active malevolence is the worst feature of human nature and the one which it is most necessary to change if the world is to grow happier. Probably this one cause has more to do with war than all the economic and political causes put together.

Given this problem of preventing malevolence, how shall we deal with it? First let us try to understand its causes. These are, I think, partly social, partly physiological. The world, now as much as at any former time, is based upon life-and-death competition; the question at issue in the War was whether German or Allied children should die of want and starvation. (Apart from malevolence on both sides there was not the slightest reason why both should not survive.) Most people have in the background of their minds a haunting fear of ruin; this is especially true of people who have children. The rich fear that Bolsheviks will confiscate their investments; the poor fear that they will lose their job or their health. Everyone is engaged in the frantic pursuit of "security" and imagines that this is to be achieved by keeping potential enemies in subjection. It is in moments of panic that cruelty becomes most widespread and most atrocious. Reactionaries everywhere appeal to fear: in England, to fear of Bolshevism; in France, to fear of Germany; in Germany, to fear of France. And the sole effect of their appeals is to increase the danger against which they wish to be protected.

It must, therefore, be one of the chief concerns of the scientific moralist to combat fear. This can be done in two ways: by increasing security, and by cultivating courage. I am speaking of fear as an irrational passion, not of the rational prevision of possible misfortune. When a theatre catches fire, the rational man foresees disaster just as clearly as the man stricken with panic, but he adopts methods likely to diminish the disaster, whereas the man stricken with panic increases it. Europe since 1914 has been like a panic-stricken audience in a theatre on fire; what is needed is calm, authoritative directions as to how to escape without trampling each other to pieces in the process. The Victorian Age, for all its humbug, was a period of rapid progress, because men were dominated by hope rather than fear. If we are again to have progress, we must again be dominated by hope.

Everything that increases the general security is likely to diminish cruelty. This applies to prevention of war, whether through the instrumentality of the League of Nations or otherwise; to prevention of destitution; to better health by improvement in medicine, hygiene, and sanitation; and to all other methods of lessening the terrors that lurk in the abysses of men's minds and emerge as nightmares when they sleep. But nothing is accomplished by an attempt to make a portion of mankind secure at the expense of another portion—Frenchmen at the expense of Germans, capitalists at the expense of wage-earners, white men at the expense of yellow men, and so on. Such methods only increase terror in the dominant group, lest just resentment should lead the oppressed to rebel. Only justice can give security; and by "justice" I mean the recognition of the equal claims of all human beings.

In addition to social changes designed to bring security there is, however, another and more direct means of diminishing fear, namely by a regimen designed to increase courage. Owing to the importance of courage in battle, men early discovered means of increasing it by education and diet—eating human flesh, for example, was supposed to be useful. But military courage was to be the prerogative of the ruling caste: Spartans were to have more than helots, British officers than Indian privates, men than women, and so on. For centuries it was supposed to be the privilege of the aristocracy. Every increase of courage in the ruling caste was used to increase the burdens on the oppressed, and therefore to increase the grounds for fear in the oppressors, and therefore to leave the causes of cruelty undiminished. Courage must be democratised before it can make men humane.

To a great extent, courage has already been democratised by recent events. The suffragettes showed that they possessed as much courage as the bravest men; this demonstration was essential in winning them the vote. The common soldier in the War needed as much courage as a captain or lieutenant, and much more than a general; this had much to do with his lack of servility after demobilisation. The Bolsheviks, who proclaim themselves the champions of the proletariat, are not lacking in courage, whatever else may be said of them; this is proved by their pre-revolutionary record. In Japan, where formerly the Samurai had a monopoly of martial ardour, conscription brought the need of courage throughout the male population. Thus among all the Great Powers much has been done during the past half-century to make courage no longer an aristocratic monopoly: if this were not the case, the danger to democracy would be far greater than it is.

But courage in fighting is by no means the only form, nor perhaps even the most important. There is courage in facing poverty, courage in facing derision, courage in facing the hostility of one's own herd. In these, the bravest soldiers are often lamentably deficient. And above all there is the courage to think calmly and rationally in the face of danger, and to control the impulse of panic fear or panic rage. These are certainly things which education can help to give. And the teaching of every form of courage is rendered easier by good health, good physique, adequate nourishment, and free play for fundamental vital impulses. Perhaps the physiological sources of courage could be discovered by comparing the blood of a cat with that of a rabbit. In all likelihood there is no limit to what science could do in the way of increasing courage, by example, experience of danger, an athletic life, and a suitable diet. All these things our upper class boys to a great extent enjoy, but as yet they are in the main the prerogative of wealth. The courage so far encouraged in the poorer sections of the community is courage under orders, not the kind that involves initiative and leadership. When the qualities that now confer leadership have become universal, there will no longer be leaders and followers, and democracy will have been realised at last.

But fear is not the only source of malevolence; envy and disappointment also have their share. The envy of cripples and hunchbacks is proverbial as a source of malignity, but other misfortunes than theirs produce similar results. A man or woman who has been thwarted sexually is apt to be full of envy; this generally takes the form of moral condemnation of the more fortunate. Much of the driving force of revolutionary movements is due to envy of the rich. Jealousy is, of course, a special form of envy—envy of love. The old often envy the young; when they do, they are apt to treat them cruelly.

There is, so far as I know, no way of dealing with envy except to make the lives of the envious happier and fuller, and to encourage in youth the idea of collective enterprises rather than competition. The worst forms of envy are in those who have not had a full life in the way of marriage, or children, or career. Such misfortunes could in most cases be avoided by better social institutions. Still, it must be admitted that a residuum of envy is likely to remain. There are many instances in history of generals so jealous of each other that they preferred defeat to enhancement of the other's reputation. Two politicians of the same party, or two artists of the same school, are almost sure to be jealous of one another. In such cases, there seems nothing to be done except to arrange, as far as possible, that each competitor shall be unable to injure the other, and shall only be able to win by superior merit. An artist's jealousy of a rival does little harm usually, because the only effective way of indulging it is to paint better pictures than his rival's, since it is not open to him to destroy his rival's pictures. Where envy is unavoidable it must be used as a stimulus to one's own efforts, not to the thwarting of the efforts of rivals.

The possibilities of science in the way of increasing human happiness are not confined to diminishing those aspects of human nature which make for mutual defeat, and which we therefore call "bad." There is probably no limit to what science can do in the way of increasing positive excellence. Health has already been greatly improved; in spite of the lamentations of those who idealise the past, we live longer and have fewer illnesses than any class or nation in the eighteenth century. With a little more application of the knowledge we already possess, we might be much healthier than we are. And future discoveries are likely to accelerate this process enormously.

So far, it has been physical science that has had most effect upon our lives, but in the future physiology and psychology are likely to be far more potent. When we have discovered how character depends upon physiological conditions, we shall be able, if we choose, to produce far more of the type of human being that we admire. Intelligence, artistic capacity, benevolence—all these things no doubt could be increased by science. There seems scarcely any limit to what could be done in the way of producing a good world, if only men would use science wisely. I have expressed elsewhere my fears that men may not make a wise use of the power they derive from science.[2] At present I am concerned with the good that men could do if they chose, not with the question whether they will choose rather to do harm.

There is a certain attitude about the application of science to human life with which I have some sympathy, though I do not, in the last analysis, agree with it. It is the attitude

---

2 See *Icarus.*

of those who dread what is "unnatural" Rousseau is, of course, the great protagonist of this view in Europe. In Asia, Lao-Tze has set it forth even more persuasively, and 2400 years sooner. I think there is a mixture of truth and falsehood in the admiration of "nature," which it is important to disentangle. To begin with, what is "natural"? Roughly speaking, anything to which the speaker was accustomed in childhood. Lao-Tze objects to roads and carriages and boats, all of which were probably unknown in the village where he was born. Rousseau has got used to these things, and does not regard them as against nature. But he would no doubt have thundered against railways if he had lived to see them. Clothes and cooking are too ancient to be denounced by most of the apostles of nature, though they all object to new fashions in either. Birth control is thought wicked by people who tolerate celibacy, because the former is a new violation of nature and the latter an ancient one. In all these ways those who preach "nature" are inconsistent, and one is tempted to regard them as mere conservatives.

Nevertheless, there is something to be said in their favour. Take for instance vitamins, the discovery of which has produced a revulsion in favour of "natural" foods. It seems, however, that vitamins can be supplied by cod liver oil and electric light, which are certainly not part of the "natural" diet of a human being. This case illustrates that, in the absence of knowledge, unexpected harm may be done by a new departure from nature; but when the harm has come to be understood it can usually be remedied by some new artificiality. As regards our physical environment and our physical means of gratifying our desires, I do not think the doctrine of "nature" justifies anything beyond a certain experimental caution in the adoption of new expedients. Clothes, for instance, are contrary to nature, and need to be supplemented by another unnatural practice, namely

washing, if they are not to bring disease. But the two practices together make a man healthier than the savage who
eschews both.

There is more to be said for "nature" in the realm of
human desires. To force upon man, woman or child a life
which thwarts their strongest impulses is both cruel and
dangerous; in this sense, a life according to "nature" is to
be commended with certain provisos. Nothing could be
more artificial than an underground electric railway, but
no violence is done to a child's nature when it is taken
to travel in one; on the contrary, almost all children find
the experience delightful. Artificialities which gratify the
desires of ordinary human beings are good, other things
being equal. But there is nothing to be said for ways of
life which are artificial in the sense of being imposed by
authority or economic necessity. Such ways of life are, no
doubt, to some extent necessary at present; ocean travel
would become very difficult if there were no stokers on
steamers. But necessities of this kind are regrettable, and
we ought to look for ways of avoiding them. A certain
amount of work is not a thing to complain of; indeed, in
nine cases out often, it makes a man happier than complete
idleness. But the amount and kind of work that most people
have to do at present is a grave evil: especially bad is the
life-long bondage to routine. Life should not be too closely
regulated or too methodical; our impulses, when not posi-
tively destructive or injurious to others, ought if possible to
have free play; there should be room for adventure. Human
nature we should respect, because our impulses and desires
are the stuff out of which our happiness is to be made. It
is no use to give men something abstractedly considered
"good"; we must give them something desired or needed if
we are to add to their happiness. Science may learn in time
to mould our desires so that they shall not conflict with

those of other people to the same extent as they do now; then we shall be able to satisfy a larger proportion of our desires than at present. In that sense, but in that sense only, our desires will then have become "better." A single desire is no better and no worse, considered in isolation, than any other; but a group of desires is better than another group if all of the first group can be satisfied simultaneously, while in the second group some are inconsistent with others. That is why love is better than hatred.

To respect physical nature is foolish; physical nature should be studied with a view to making it serve human ends as far as possible, but it remains ethically neither good nor bad. And where physical nature and human nature interact, as in the population question, there is no need to fold our hands in passive adoration and accept war, pestilence and famine as the only possible means of dealing with excessive fertility. The divines say: it is wicked, in this matter, to apply science to the physical side of the problem; we must (they say) apply morals to the human side and practise abstinence. Apart from the fact that everyone, including the divines, knows that their advice will not be taken, why should it be wicked to solve the population question by adopting physical means for preventing conception? No answer is forthcoming except one based upon antiquated dogmas. And clearly the violence to nature advocated by the divines is at least as great as that involved in birth control. The divines prefer a violence to human nature, which, when successfully practised, involves unhappiness, envy, a tendency to persecution, often madness. I prefer a "violence" to physical nature which is of the same sort as that involved in the steam engine or even in the use of an umbrella. This instance shows how ambiguous and uncertain is the application of the principle that we should follow "nature."

Nature, even human nature, will cease more and more to be an absolute datum; more and more it will become what scientific manipulation has made it. Science can, if it chooses, enable our grandchildren to live the good life, by giving them knowledge, self-control, and characters productive of harmony rather than strife. At present it is teaching our children to kill each other, because many men of science are willing to sacrifice the future of mankind to their own momentary prosperity. But this phase will pass when men have acquired the same domination over their own passions that they already have over the physical forces of the external world. Then at last we shall have won our freedom.

BIOGRAPHICAL TIMELINE

1872   Bertrand Arthur William Russell (3rd Earl Russell) is born on May 18 in Trellech, Monmouthshire, Wales, into an influential aristocratic family. He is the son of Viscount and Viscountess Amberley, who are radical for their time. His father, Lord Amberley, is known for his unorthodox views on religion and for his active support of birth control and women's suffrage, which contributed to the end of his short career as Liberal Member of Parliament. His mother, Lady Amberley, is a British suffragist and an early advocate of birth control in the United Kingdom. With her husband's consent, she has an affair with her children's tutor, the biologist Douglas Spalding. Russell is the godson of John Stuart Mill and the grandson of Lord John Russell (1st Earl), prime minister to Queen Victoria in the 1840s and 1860s. He has two siblings: a brother, Frank, who is seven years older and a sister, Rachel, who is four years older.

1874   Mother dies of diphtheria; sister Rachel's dies shortly thereafter.

1876   Father dies of bronchitis after a long depression. Russell, age four, and his older brother Frank move in with their rigidly Victorian grandparents (former Prime Minister Earl Russell and Countess Russell) in Richmond Park, London.

1883   Develops a passionate interest in mathematics after being introduced to Euclid by his brother Frank, an event that he describes in his autobiography as "one of the great events of my life, as dazzling as first love."

1887   Grandfather Lord John Russell dies, leaving the children entirely in the care of their grandmother, Countess Russell, a devout Scottish Presbyterian who successfully petitions the court to set aside a provision in Amberley's will requiring the children to be raised as agnostics. At this time, begins to doubt the validity of Christian religious dogma.

1889   Meets future wife Alys Pearsall Smith, an American Quaker five years his elder and a graduate of Bryn Mawr College near Philadelphia.

1890   Becomes an atheist after reading Mill's *Autobiography*.

        Travels to European continent and visits the Eiffel Tower.

        Wins a scholarship to study mathematics at Trinity College, Cambridge. While at Cambridge, meets future co-author of *Principia Mathematica,* Alfred North Whitehead, and George Edward Moore, who would become a long-time collaborator.

1893   Graduates with a first-class B.A. in mathematics.

1894   Completes the Moral Sciences Tripos at Cambridge.

        Marries Alys Pearsall Smith on December 13.

1896   Publishes first work, *German Social Democracy.*

Teaches German social democracy at the London School of Economics.

1895   Studies at the University of Berlin.

1896   Appointed lecturer at the London School of Economics; lectures in the US at Johns Hopkins and Bryn Mawr.

1897   *An Essay on the Foundations of Geometry.*

1899   Appointed lecturer at Trinity College, Cambridge.

1900   *A Critical Exposition of the Philosophy of Leibniz.*

Attends the First International Congress of Philosophy in Paris and meets Giuseppe Peano whose *Formulario mathematico* is instrumental in his formulation of Russell's paradox, which he publishes the following year.

1901   Marriage to Alys Pearsall Smith begins to fall apart.

1903   Advances the famous paradox bearing his name in his work *The Principles of Mathematics;* publishes *A Free Man's Worship, and Other Essays.*

1905   Introduces the theory of descriptions in "On Denoting," which is published in the philosophical journal *Mind.*

1907   Advocates, as a candidate for Parliament, for women's suffrage. Does not win election.

1908   Elected a Fellow of the Royal Society.

1910   *Philosophical Essays;* also publishes, with Alfred North Whitehead, the three-volume *Principia Mathematica* (1910–13).

Reappointed lecturer at Trinity College, Cambridge;

is passed over for a Fellowship because of his "anti-clerical" views. Teaches and mentors Ludwig Wittgenstein.

1911   Separates from Alys Pearsall Smith; begins affair with Lady Ottoline Morrell, a society hostess and patron of writers such as Aldous Huxley, Siegfried Sassoon, T. S. Eliot, and D. H. Lawrence, and artists including Mark Gertler, Dora Carrington, and Gilbert Spencer. Also has simultaneous affairs with a number of other women, including, according to some, Vivienne Haigh-Wood, the English governess and writer, and first wife of T. S. Eliot.

1912   *The Problems of Philosophy.*

1913   Lectures at the École des Hautes Sociales in Paris.

1914   *Our Knowledge of the External World as a Field for Scientific Method in Philosophy.*

Visits Harvard and teaches courses in logic and the theory of knowledge; meets T. S. Eliot.

1916   *Principles of Social Reconstruction; Why Men Fight; Justice in War-time.*

Dismissed from Trinity College for passivist stance and agitating against British involvement in World War I, for which he is convicted under the Defence of the Realm Act 1914.

1917   *Political Ideals.*

Plays a significant part in the Leeds Convention in June, a gathering of well over a thousand "anti-war socialists." Including delegates from the Independent Labour Party and the Socialist Party, united in their pacifist beliefs and advocating a peace settlement.

1918   "The Philosophy of Logical Atomism" (a series

of eight lectures); *Mysticism and Logic and Other Essays; Proposed Roads to Freedom: Socialism, Anarchism, and Syndicalism.*

Convicted and imprisoned for five months for lecturing against inviting the United States to enter the war on the United Kingdom's side.

1919   *Introduction to Mathematical Philosophy.*

1920   In January, Russell accepts offer of reinstatement at Trinity College due to pressure by majority of the Fellows of the College. However, requests a yearlong leave of absence. Over the summer, visits Soviet Russia as part of an official delegation sent by the British government to investigate the effects of the Russian Revolution. Meets Vladimir Lenin and, in his autobiography, writes that he found Lenin disappointing, sensing an "impish cruelty" in him. His first-hand experiences destroy his previous tentative support for the revolution.

Publishes *The Practice and Theory of Bolshevism* in November.

1921   *The Analysis of Mind.*

In January, resigns from Trinity College due to tumultuous events in his personal life.

Russell, accompanied by his lover Dora Black, a British author, feminist, and socialist campaigner, visits Peking (now Beijing) to lecture on philosophy.

On August 26, returns to England. Dora is six months pregnant. Hastily divorces Alys Pearsall Smith and marries Dora Black on September 27.

On November 16, Dora gives birth to John Conrad Russell, 4th Earl Russell.

1922   *The Problem of China;* "Free Thought and Official Propaganda" (lecture).

Knowing he is extremely unlikely to be elected in such a safe Conservative seat, unsuccessfully stands as a Labour Party candidate for Chelsea in the House of Commons.

1923   *The Prospects of Industrial Civilization* (with Dora Russell); *The ABC of Atoms.*

Again, unsuccessfully stands as a Labour Party candidate for Chelsea in the House of Commons.

Birth of daughter Katharine Jane Russell (later Lady Katharine Tait) on December 29.

1924   *Icarus; or, The Future of Science.*

1925   *The ABC of Relativity; What I Believe.*

1926   *On Education, Especially in Early Childhood.*

Delivers *Tarner Lectures* on the Philosophy of the Sciences at Trinity College.

1927   *The Analysis of Matter; An Outline of Philosophy;* "Why I Am Not a Christian."

Co-founds the Beacon Hill School with his wife Dora Black.

1928   *Sceptical Essays.*

1929   *Marriage and Morals,* in which he advocates for equality between the sexes, no-fault divorce, expanded sexual and professional freedom for women, and other progressive social measures.

1930   *The Conquest of Happiness.*

Daughter Harriet Ruth is born on July 8.

1931   *The Scientific Outlook.*

Older brother Frank dies, thus becomes 3rd Earl Russell.

1932   *Education and the Social Order.*

Separates from Dora, who, during their marriage, had two children with American journalist, Griffin Barry.

Awarded the De Morgan Medal.

Becomes Chair of the India League, the foremost lobby in the United Kingdom for Indian independence, a position he holds until 1939.

1934   *Freedom and Organization, 1814–1914.*

Awarded the Sylvester Medal.

1935   *In Praise of Idleness and Other Essays; Religion and Science.*

Divorce from Dora.

1936   *Which Way to Peace?*

On January 18, marries third wife, Oxford undergraduate Patricia ("Peter") Spence, who had been his children's governess since 1930.

1937   Birth of son with Patricia Spence, Conrad Sebastian Robert Russell, 5th Earl Russell, who would become a prominent historian and one of the leading figures in the Liberal Democrat party.

Returns to London School of Economics to lecture on the science of power.

Opposes rearmament against Nazi Germany.

1938   *Power: A New Social Analysis.*

Appointed visiting professor of philosophy at Chicago.

1939   Appointed professor of philosophy at the University of California at Los Angeles.

1940   *An Inquiry into Meaning and Truth.*

Changes position on war with Germany and advocates defeating Hitler, who he believes poses a permanent threat to democracy in Europe.

Appointed professor at City College of New York. He is quickly dismissed, however, after a court judgment pronounces him "morally unfit" to teach at the college because of his opinions.

1941   Appointed lecturer at the Barnes Foundation in Pennsylvania.

1942   Dismissed from Barnes Foundation, but wins a lawsuit against the Foundation for wrongful dismissal.

1943   Expresses support for the creation of an Israeli state; adopts a stance toward warfare called "relative political pacifism" that holds that war, in extreme circumstances, may be the lesser of two evils.

1944   Reappointed Fellow at Trinity College.

1945   *A History of Western Philosophy; The Bomb and Civilisation.*

1948   *Human Knowledge: Its Scope and Limits.*

Is one of twenty-four survivors (among a total of forty-three passengers) of an airplane crash in Hommelvik, Norway, in October.

"Authority and the Individual" (series of six BBC broadcasts).

In a public speech at Westminster School, addressing a gathering arranged by the New Commonwealth, Russell shocks some observers by suggesting that a preemptive nuclear strike on the Soviet Union might be justified.

1949   *Authority and the Individual.*

Awarded the Order of Merit; elected a Lifetime Fellow at Trinity College.

1950   *Unpopular Essays.*

Awarded the Nobel Prize in Literature.

1951   *New Hopes for a Changing World.*

1952   *The Impact of Science on Society.*

Patricia Spence divorces Russell. On December 12, marries Edith Finch, an American writer and biographer, whom he had known since 1925.

1953   *Satan in the Suburbs and Other Stories.*

1954   *Human Society in Ethics and Politics; Nightmares of Eminent Persons and Other Stories.*

Delivers "Man's Peril" address on the BBC on December 23.

1955   Enlists Albert Einstein and numerous other luminary scientists to sign the Russell-Einstein Manifesto, which is issued on July 9. It highlights the dangers posed by nuclear weapons and calls for world leaders to seek peaceful resolutions to international conflict.

1956   *Portraits from Memory and Other Essays.*

Expresses opposition to European imperialism in the Middle East.

1957   Elected president of the first Pugwash Conference on Science and World Affairs, which drew its inspiration from the Russell-Einstein Manifesto of 1955.

1958   *Understanding History and Other Essays; The Will to Doubt.*

Founds the Campaign for Nuclear Disarmament.

1959   *Common Sense and Nuclear Warfare; My Philosophical Development.*

1961   *Fact and Fiction; Has Man a Future?*

At the age of eighty-nine, imprisoned for seven days for a "breach of the peace" after taking part in an anti-nuclear demonstration in London.

1963   *Essays in Skepticism; Unarmed Victory.*

Awarded the inaugural Jerusalem Prize; establishes the Bertrand Russell Peace Foundation.

1966   *The ABC of Relativity.*

1967   Launches the International War Crimes Tribunal.

Publishes *War Crimes in Vietnam* and a three-volume *Autobiography* beginning in 1967.

1970   On 31 January 1970, Russell issues a statement condemning "Israel's aggression in the Middle East," and in particular, Israeli bombing raids being carried out deep in Egyptian territory.

On February 2, Bertrand Russell dies of influenza in Penrhyndeudraeth, Wales, United Kingdom. His body is cremated in Colwyn Bay on February 5. In accordance with his will, there is no religious ceremony but one minute's silence; his ashes are later scattered over the Welsh mountains.

Made in the USA
Las Vegas, NV
28 June 2024